ROBERT FULTON INVENTS THE STEAMBOAT

Kate Rogers

ROSEN COMMON CORE READERS

Rosen Classroom™

New York

Published in 2014 by The Rosen Publishing Group, Inc.
29 East 21st Street, New York, NY 10010

Book Design: Michael J. Flynn

Photo Credits: Cover SuperStock/Getty Images; pp. 3–4, 6–8, 10, 12, 14, 16, 18, 20–24 (wood texture) marussia/Shutterstock.com; pp. 4, 6, 8, 10, 12, 14, 16, 18, 20–21 (steam) nikkytok/Shutterstock.com; pp. 5, 15 (Livingston) Stock Montage/Archive Photos/Getty Images; p. 7 DEA/A. DAGLI ORTI/De Agostini Picture Library/Getty Images; pp. 9 (Fulton), 17 (steamboat) Science & Society Picture Library/SSPL/Getty Images; pp. 9 (steamboat), 19 (all) courtesy of the Library of Congress; p. 11 (sloop) Kostyantyn Ivanyshen/Shutterstock.com; p. 11 (steamboat) Universal Images Group/Getty Images; p. 13 Photos.com/Thinkstock.com; p. 15 DEA PICTURE LIBRARY/De Agostini Picture Library/Getty Images; p. 17 (map) Olinchuk/Shutterstock.com; p. 20 (Fulton) Nicku/Shutterstock.com.

ISBN: 978-1-4777-2603-7
6-pack ISBN: 978-1-4777-2604-4

Manufactured in the United States of America

CPSIA Compliance Information: Batch #CS13RC: For further information contact Rosen Publishing, New York, New York at 1-800-237-9932.

CONTENTS

A GREAT INVENTOR

Eva wants to be an inventor someday. She wants to learn more about important inventors in American history. Her teacher, Miss Jackson, says, "You should learn more about Robert Fulton, the man who invented the first **commercially** successful steamboat. His invention changed American life!"

Eva learns that Robert Fulton was born on November 14, 1765, in Lancaster County, Pennsylvania. He's best known as the inventor of the steamboat, which is a boat that runs on steam power. He was also an **engineer** and artist!

Eva asks, "How did Robert Fulton become an inventor?" She can't wait to learn more about him!

YOUNG ROBERT FULTON

Fulton grew up in the Pennsylvania countryside. His parents were from Ireland. His father owned a farm. Unfortunately, his father wasn't successful and lost the farm when Fulton was a young boy.

Miss Jackson says, "In the 1700s, young men were often sent to be an **apprentice** at a business. It was an opportunity to learn a skill." At age 17, Fulton was sent to be an apprentice in a **jewelry** shop in Philadelphia. His job was to paint tiny pictures on rings and necklaces.

Fulton painted jewelry like this.
After working at the jewelry shop, he decided
he wanted to be a painter.

Many people who saw Fulton's paintings thought he was very talented. By 1786, he earned enough money from painting to buy a small farm for his mother. When Fulton returned to Philadelphia, local business owners agreed to give him money to go to London. Many great painters lived there.

"Why isn't Robert Fulton known as a great artist?" Eva asks. Miss Jackson explains that many people in London liked Fulton's paintings, but didn't think they were worth very much money.

With little success in painting, Fulton discovered another interest: new inventions for water travel.

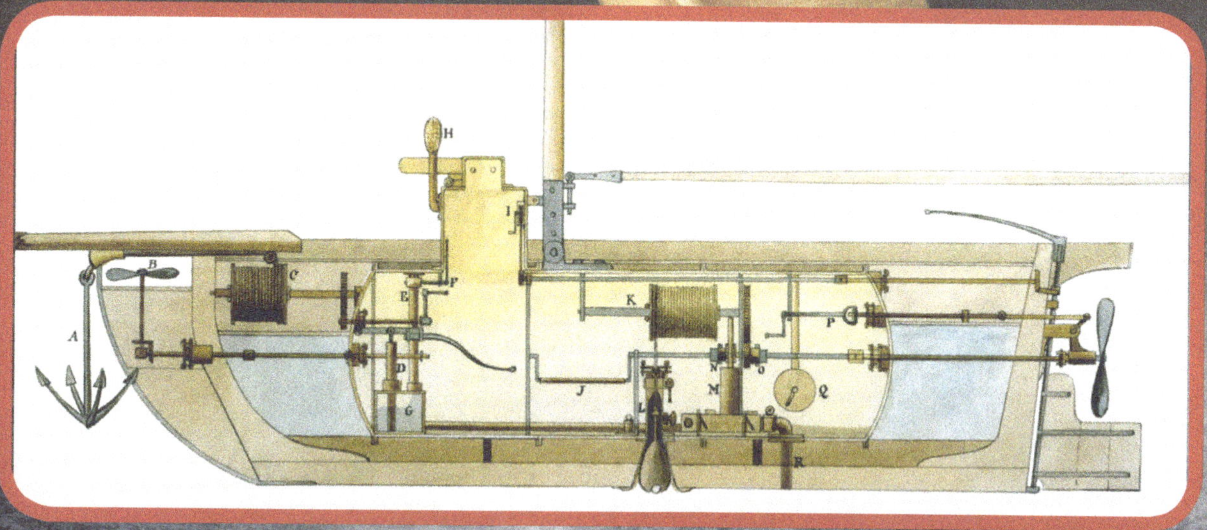

WHAT ARE STEAMBOATS?

Fulton was excited to learn about new boats called steamboats. Inventor John Fitch built the first one in 1787, but it had many problems and wasn't commercially successful. Eva asks, "How do steamboats work?"

Miss Jackson explains that steam is water that's heated until it turns into gas. The steam creates pressure in the engine and moves parts that push the boat forward. Robert did experiments to learn how steamboats could be improved. He thought they needed more paddles, or wheels that move a boat forward or backward.

Before steamboats, goods were often carried in sloops, or boats with long sails. Steamboats moved faster and didn't depend on wind.

STEAMBOAT
SLOOP

Fulton was very interested in water travel and, most importantly, shipping. People were still in need of an easy way to **transport** goods from one place to another. It was easy to transport things to ports, or towns on the water, but what about towns inland?

Fulton became interested in canal engineering, or building man-made waterways. In 1796, he wrote a book that planned a system of canals through the countryside and explained the benefits of canal transport.

Canals allow boats to carry goods and people farther inland. This is a picture from Fulton's book about canals.

ROBERT'S INVENTIONS

Fulton's ideas and inventions weren't always taken seriously. Few people paid any attention to his canal ideas. In 1797, he went to France with ideas for a submarine that could attack other boats. The French government wasn't very interested.

Meanwhile, Fulton was still thinking about steamboats. In 1801, he met Robert R. Livingston, a man who had been in the steamboat business for many years. They became business partners and decided they'd both pay to build Fulton's new steamboat **design**.

"Why was Fulton's design special?" Eva asks. The design called for a side paddlewheel and a powerful engine. Livingston thought it was a great idea!

ROBERT R.
LIVINGSTON

Miss Jackson says, "Fulton's first design didn't work, but he didn't give up!" In 1806, a crew started constructing his new steamboat design in New York. A few months later, it was ready!

Fulton's steamboat was 150 feet (46 m) long, and it had a paddlewheel on each side. He took his steamboat on a **trial** run from New York City to Albany. It took his boat only 32 hours to go a distance of 150 miles (240 km). It took other boats nearly four days to go that far!

"How fast did Fulton's steamboat travel?" Eva asks. "Almost five miles per hour," Miss Jackson says.

ALBANY
NEW YORK
Hudson River
NEW YORK CITY

A SUCCESSFUL STEAMBOAT

After the successful trial run, Fulton kept improving his steamboat. He added an engine house, short walls around the deck, and cabins for people to stay in. He named the boat the *North River Steamboat*. It was very successful!

Fulton's steamboat made three trips back and forth between New York City and Albany every two weeks. His fast steamboat could carry both goods and people. He kept making improvements until it looked like a whole new boat! It was officially named the *North River Steamboat of Clermont* in 1808.

Eva learns that newspapers called Fulton's steamboat *Clermont* for short. It was the first steamboat to successfully carry many people and goods.

CLERMONT

The year 1808 was a busy one for Fulton! He had a successful steamboat, and he also married Livingston's niece, Harriet. Soon after, he designed a new steamboat called the *New Orleans*. It became the first steamboat to travel in the waters of the western United States.

After the *Clermont's* success, other people used Fulton's design. Soon steamboats were common modes of transportation. Throughout the 1800s, as steamboats improved, they were used for cheap, easy travel up and down the Mississippi River.

Miss Jackson says, "Here are some important events that happened in the history of steamboats!"

STEAMBOAT HISTORY

1765	Scottish inventor James Watt invents the first steam engine.
1775	Matthew Boulton, an English engineer, pays to build Watt's steam engine.
1787	John Fitch, an American inventor, builds a steamboat and sails on the Delaware River.
1807	Robert Fulton's steamboat, *Clermont*, travels up the Hudson River. It becomes the first commercially successful steamboat.
1811	The *New Orleans* is the first steamboat to travel the western waters of the United States.
1819	The *Savannah* becomes the first steamboat to cross the Atlantic Ocean.
1883	Famous American author Mark Twain writes *Life on the Mississippi*, a book about his years as a steamboat pilot.
1928	Walt Disney's Mickey Mouse stars in the movie *Steamboat Willie* as a steamboat pilot.

THE BEST THING

Robert Fulton is best known for inventing a successful steamboat, but he invented and engineered other things, too. He supported the building of the Erie Canal, which was an important waterway connecting Albany to Buffalo. He also designed a steamship and submarines to be used in war.

Fulton died on February 24, 1815, in New York City. He never grew very rich from his inventions, but his steamboat design helped change inland water travel forever. "The best thing about Robert Fulton," Eva says, "is that he never gave up!"

GLOSSARY

apprentice (uh-PREHN-tuhs) Someone who works for somebody else to learn a skill or trade.

commercial (kuh-MUHR-shuhl) Having to do with making money.

design (dih-ZYN) A plan or outline showing how something is to be built.

engineer (ehn-juh-NIHR) Someone who is trained in the use or building of machines.

jewelry (JOOL-ree) Rings, watches, necklaces, and other pretty things worn on the body.

transport (TRANS-pohrt) To carry from one place to another.

trial (TRY-uhl) The act or process of testing.

INDEX